＊

MARGARET WITHERS

Margaret Withers took up her role as the Archbishop's Officer for Evangelism among Children in June 2001. Formerly Children's Work Adviser for the Diocese of Rochester, she taught in several Inner London schools and for the Open University before becoming a Diocesan Children's Adviser in 1989. During her years as a Diocesan Adviser, she became heavily involved in providing training and support for voluntary children's leaders in parishes. In 1996, while Children's Officer for the diocese of Chelmsford, she established children's work as an integral part of Reader training as well as providing a similar input to several theological courses. The increasing demand for simple basic training for inexperienced leaders led to her writing a four-evening course for a group of parishes in 1998. This formed the basis of her book, Fired up... not burnt out, *which was published under BRF's Barnabas imprint in 2001. She is also author of* The Amazing Book of Acts *and* Welcome to the Lord's Table, *both also published under the Barnabas imprint.*

Text copyright © Margaret Withers 2003
The author asserts the moral right
to be identified as the author of this work

Published by
The Bible Reading Fellowship
First Floor, Elsfield Hall
15–17 Elsfield Way, Oxford OX2 8FG
ISBN 1 84101 208 4

First published 2003
10 9 8 7 6 5 4 3 2 1 0

Acknowledgments
Unless otherwise stated, scripture quotations are taken from the Good News
Bible published by The Bible Societies/HarperCollins Publishers Ltd, UK ©
American Bible Society 1966, 1971, 1976, 1992, used with permission.

Prayers and extracts from *Common Worship: Initiation Services* (Church House
Publishing 1998) are copyright © The Central Board of Finance of the
Church of England, 1997, 1998; The Archbishops' Council, 1999, and are
reproduced by permission.

p. 61: 'Pattern of Life' by John Oxenham is used by permission of
Desmond Dunkerley.

A catalogue record for this book is available from the British Library

Printed and bound in Great Britain by
Bookmarque, Croydon

THE GIFTS OF

Baptism

An essential guide for parents, sponsors & leaders

✳

MARGARET WITHERS

In memory of
Deirdre Gillies,
an exceptional godmother
and a good friend

PREFACE

A child is going to be baptized. You may be that child's parent or you may have been asked to be a godparent or sponsor. You want to know a little about what baptism means so that you can take a more active part. Maybe you have recently been present at a baptism and your children are asking you about the things that took place.

This little book takes you through the baptism service by following the journey of Joe and his baby sister, Amy, as they prepare to be baptized. Baptism is a sacrament, an outward sign of God's grace, his generous love, at work in our lives, so signs and symbols play a large part in the service. Each chapter introduces and discusses them alongside some of the text and prayers from the service. It also uses short extracts from the Bible to describe the ways that people have seen themselves as belonging to God their creator, and the new life that Jesus promised to all who follow him.

If you are talking to children who are going to be present at a baptism, you will find special sections geared towards their age groups. These sections could be used separately with children in a church group as well as within a family.

The baptism service is rich in its use of signs of God's saving love—water, oil, light, and so on. Each chapter starts with two sections, 'Preparation' and 'Thinking about…', which suggest that you collect some everyday articles to help with your thinking and discussion. Do not be tempted to skip these sections. They provide a vital link between your daily life and the service, as well as helping you to think about the practical uses and their symbolic meaning. Clergy and other leaders could easily adapt these sections for use as a preparation course for a group of parents.

If you are a parent or godparent, read a little of this book at a time and be prepared to ask questions of someone connected with the church if you are uncertain about anything. Baptism is a first step on a lifelong journey. You are helping a child to take these first steps with confidence and to grow in knowledge and love of Jesus, who said, 'Follow me.'

CONTENTS

FOREWORD

When invited to a baptism or christening, many people wonder if they should bring a gift—and, if so, what? Godparents worry about it and are often unsure of their role both in the service and in the life of their godchild. And parents can find themselves in a muddle on how and whom to choose to be their child's godparents.

The greatest gift to offer any child is your prayers. The best godparent a child can have is a friend who thinks about them and brings those thoughts to God. Praying for children as they grow up consciously places the child within the embrace of God's love.

At the heart of my Bishop's ring is an amethyst that belonged to my great-aunt. It wasn't until I was an adult that I learnt that she had prayed for me every day of my life since my baptism as an infant. Although I do not fully understand this, I believe that her prayers were formative in my decision to turn to Christ. Jesus welcomes infants as children of his kingdom. He literally took them in his arms.

In this book, Margaret Withers helps us to see how baptism is an extension of that embrace of Jesus Christ.

I pray that those who read this book and bring a child to baptism will be faithful in praying for them so that they in turn may grow up to follow Jesus Christ.

The Rt Revd James Jones
Bishop of Liverpool

THE GIFT OF BAPTISM

WETTING THE BABY'S HEAD

Joe was so excited when Amy was born. Joe was nearly four and felt very grown up now he had a baby sister. He loved showing her off at St Mary's preschool in the church hall, and seeing her bathed and fed. Joe was not the only child in the preschool to have a baby sister. His friend Jason's sister, Daisy, was born the same week as Amy.

One day, Jason's mum handed Joe's mum a card. *'We are wetting the baby's head on Sunday, at St Mary's at 10 o'clock. Do come.'*

So, on Sunday morning, Joe and Amy put on their best clothes and went with their parents to St Mary's church. They were invited to sit near the back so that they could see Daisy baptized at the font, a big bowl by the church door. Joe watched carefully as Daisy had a cross marked on her forehead with oil. Then a man dressed in a long white robe took Daisy in his arms. He poured water over her head three times, saying, *'Daisy, I baptize you in the name of the Father, and of the Son, and of the Holy Spirit.'* Everyone shouted, 'Amen'. Then Daisy's dad was given a candle to hold and everyone clapped.

Joe was not quite sure what had happened. There had been a lot of talking and some singing. The man had talked about how Jesus loved children. Joe had seen pictures of Jesus and a cross on the wall in the church hall, but he did not know who Jesus was. He had asked Dad a lot of questions starting with 'Why...', but Dad did not give very good answers. It had been a lovely day and everyone had been happy. Joe looked at his baby sister, Amy, asleep in her crib. Joe went to find his mother. 'Mum,' he said, 'is Amy going to have water on her head like Daisy?' Joe's mum looked at him quietly for a minute, and said, 'Well, perhaps she should. But Joe, you have not been baptized either. Next time you go to preschool I'll ask Carol, the leader, what we should do.'

JOE AND AMY ARE GOING TO BE BAPTIZED

Joe's family had been invited to see Daisy baptized. Now Joe and Amy were also going to be baptized. Joe had just had his fourth birthday and Amy was about six months old. Carol, the preschool leader, arranged for the vicar to call at their home. He helped Joe and Amy's parents to understand something of the meaning of baptism. He explained how, in the ceremony, simple everyday things like water and oil are used but have a special meaning. He talked about God's love for everyone. He explained how they must promise to help Joe and Amy to be Christians—followers of Jesus Christ.

THE BAPTISM SERVICE

Joe and Amy's parents wanted the baptism to be a real celebration, so they invited their family and friends to the service. At the vicar's suggestion, they went to the church on several Sundays and had a rehearsal there with Joe and Amy's godparents on the evening before the service. After the service, they had a party at home. Jason and Daisy's family was invited. 'After all,' said Joe, 'it's because of Daisy that this is happening.'

YOUR CHILD'S BAPTISM

You are also involved in the baptism of a child. You may be that child's parent or you may have been asked to be a godparent or sponsor. You also want to know a little about what baptism means. You may want to explain about baptism to the children in your family or at your church. The child may be a baby like Amy or an older child like Joe. In this book, we are going to explore the baptism service by following their baptism.

Your child's baptism will also be a special occasion for you and your family and friends. You will meet in church. This may be your local church that you have attended many times. If you are not familiar with it, though, see that you visit it and attend some services. This will put you at ease and help you to find out more about what it means to be part of the Church, God's family.

During the baptism service, familiar articles like water, oil and candles will be used. They all have symbolic meanings that have developed over the centuries. Afterwards you may have a party and there are sure to be presents. This is all part of celebrating the newest addition to the family, but it is also about welcoming the child as a new Christian, part of God's family.

THE MEANING OF THE SERVICE

The service may be unfamiliar. This book will tell you more about the baptism service, and the meaning of the various signs and symbols in it. Each chapter concerns a section in the service. It relates that section of the service to objects and events that belong to everyday life, to help everyone to understand something of the wonder and mystery behind the actions and words. Baptism is a 'sacrament'—an outward sign of God acting in our lives. Amy is too young to know what is happening, but Joe is old enough for his parents to teach him a little about God and about the service. They can also read stories about Jesus to him. He may start to go to the Sunday Club at St Mary's church with his friend, Jason.

Whether your children are going to be baptized or are going to a baptism as visitors, take the opportunity to tell them about it. There are suggestions headed 'Talking with Joe' in each of the following chapters. Talk to your family and the child's godparents or let them have a copy of this book. If you are meeting as a group, use the various visual aids suggested at the beginning of each session.

This is how the chapters in this book link with the sections of the baptism service:

Chapter	Section of service
1. The gift of a child	Presentation
2. The gift of light	Decision
3. The gift of the cross	Signing with the cross
4. The gift of water	Prayer over the water
5. The gift of faith	Profession of faith
6. The gift of new life	Baptism
7. The gift of glory	Commission
8. The gift of the Church	Welcome
Postscript: The gift of the world	Sending out

GOD'S ACTS!

At the same time as all this is taking place in the service, other things will be happening that you cannot see or hear. God will act in Joe and Amy's lives as they are baptized. He will also act in your child's life. His love and generosity are limitless. The word we often use for these qualities is 'grace'. God has already given you the gift of a child. Now he will give his grace to that child through the gift of baptism.

PRAYER

May God who has received you by baptism into his Church
pour upon you the riches of his grace,
that within the company of Christ's pilgrim people
you may daily be renewed by his anointing Spirit,
and come to the inheritance of the saints in glory. Amen

COMMON WORSHIP: PRAYER AFTER BAPTISM

Chapter One

THE GIFT OF A CHILD

PREPARATION

This chapter is about giving and receiving gifts. To aid your thinking and discussion, quickly wrap a few objects as if they were gifts. Include an electrical appliance like a hair-drier. If you are talking about this chapter with children, include an electronic toy like a keyboard or a car. See that each child has something to unwrap. Things that have to be made or used, like models or pencil sharpeners, are especially suitable.

THINKING ABOUT GIFTS

Being given presents is great fun. First, there is the package wrapped in coloured paper, maybe with ribbons and a label.

Pick up a giftwrapped parcel. How does the paper feel? When you squeeze it, is the parcel hard or soft? Gifts like books and CDs are hard to disguise, but even if the shape gives the contents away, the title remains a mystery.

It is only when we unwrap the package that we can really

appreciate the gift. With some gifts, we may need additional objects or guidance to enjoy them fully—electrical power points, an instruction book or even a relation or friend to help us to use the gift.

Joe and Amy's parents have asked God for a gift—the gift of baptism. To make the most of this gift, they will need to unwrap it and enjoy it. It is the same for you. Suppose you receive an electrical appliance as a gift. You can plug in to God's love, just like plugging in an electrical appliance, but you need to turn on the switch and learn how to respond to this love.

Giving presents is just as much fun as receiving them. First, there is the choosing, then the wrapping. The tense moment is when you hand over the gift. Will it be acceptable; will it give pleasure?

Baptism is about giving as well as receiving. Joe and Amy's parents are offering their children back to God. Joe and Amy are becoming members of God's family, the Church. That is why most baptism services take place within a Sunday service or with representatives of the congregation present. When you go to your baptism service, people from the church will welcome you, your family and friends and, most of all, the new member of God's family. You may feel rather tense when it comes to the service. One thing you can know is that God's love is unconditional. There is no question of whether your gift will be acceptable. God accepts all that you offer.

THINK OR DISCUSS

- What do you enjoy about giving and receiving presents?
- Can you think of a present for which you needed help in order to use and enjoy it?
- How can you see the generosity of God in your own life?

SCRIPTURE READING

This story was written several thousand years ago, but the message is still clear today. It is about a woman who longed for a child. Her grief was exacerbated by the scorn of her rival within the household who had several children. Samuel was God's gift to an oppressed woman. His life was God's gift; in return, his mother offered his life back to God.

There was a man named Elkanah, from the tribe of Ephraim, who lived in the town of Ramah in the hill country of Ephraim. Elkanah had two wives, Hannah and Peninnah. Peninnah had children but Hannah had none.

One day, after they had finished their meal in the house of the Lord at Shiloh, Hannah got up. She was deeply distressed, and she cried bitterly as she prayed to the Lord. Meanwhile, Eli the priest was sitting in his place by the door. Hannah made a solemn promise: 'Almighty Lord, look at me, your servant! See my trouble and remember me! Do not forget me! If you give me a son, I promise that I will dedicate him to you for his whole life.'

So it was that she became pregnant and gave birth to a son. She named him Samuel, and explained, 'I asked the Lord for him.' After Samuel was weaned, Hannah took him to Eli the priest at Shiloh. Hannah said to him, 'Excuse me, sir. Do you remember me? I am the woman you saw standing here, praying to the Lord. I asked him for this child, and he gave me what I asked for. So I am dedicating him to the Lord. As long as he lives, he will belong to the Lord.'

BASED ON 1 SAMUEL 1:1–28

The story continues with Hannah's song of joy at God's love and generosity to her. Later, Samuel became a great leader and prophet, whom God used to do great and wonderful things in his nation of Israel.

TALKING ABOUT GIFTS WITH CHILDREN

Start by asking when we receive presents. Invite each child to choose a parcel. Ask the children to guess what is in the parcels by feeling them. Point out that we have to unwrap a gift before we can find out what it is. Then we see the title of the book, or the colour of the pen, and so on. With some gifts, like games and models, we need to be shown how to use them properly.

Now look at the electronic toy. Ask how it should be used. Draw out the idea that it needs to be plugged into the power point or fitted with a battery and then switched on before it is any use.

Ask about giving presents. Is it fun choosing them? What do people say when they receive them?

We are looking forward to Joe and Amy being baptized. God will be showing his love for them. For Joe and Amy, it will be like being given a present. We will also be offering Joe and Amy back to God. They will become part of God's family of Christians all over the world. As they get older, we will show them what it means to be a Christian.

QUESTIONS AND ANSWERS

- Do you enjoy giving and receiving presents?
- Do you need help with using some presents?
- What things has God given you?

SCRIPTURE READING

Tell the story of Samuel's birth, from the text above, or in your own words, or by using a child's version of the story.

✽

TALKING WITH JOE

This wording could be used when talking to a young child about a baby who is going to be baptized.

Joe, what is good about having a baby sister? Amy was a very special present. We are going to thank God for her, and for you, when you are both baptized.

✽

IN THE SERVICE

THE PRESENTATION

When Joe and Amy are baptized, the vicar leading the service will welcome them with their family and friends at the beginning of the service. Later in the service, he will ask if the people present will welcome Joe and Amy and sustain them in their new life after baptism. Then he asks the parents and godparents if they will help Joe and Amy to grow in faith through prayer, example and support.

A few minutes after the baptism, everyone present will greet Joe and Amy by saying:

We welcome you into the fellowship of faith;
We are children of the same heavenly Father;
We welcome you.

You may find that seats have been reserved for you near the front of the church or by the font. Your names may be on the service sheet. You and your family will be mentioned in the prayers and your children will be formally welcomed after the baptism. This is to help you to know that the whole Christian community is there to support you.

AFTER THE BAPTISM

We have to take care of our gifts. Pray for your child and say prayers with him or her. You may find this difficult. The priest or minister who led the baptism is there to help you, or you may like to ask a friend in the congregation. Bring your child to church sometimes. There will probably be a service that is geared towards children, or you may feel happier at a pram service or a parent and toddler group. Each church is different but, wherever you live, you should find one that welcomes young families and at which you feel at ease.

PRAYER

Thou who hast given so much to me,
Give one thing more,
A grateful heart,
For Christ's sake, Amen.

GEORGE HERBERT (1593–1633)

Chapter Two

THE GIFT OF LIGHT

PREPARATION

One of the strongest images in the baptism service is the idea of living in darkness and then moving into the light. Collect items that remind you of light and darkness—for example, candles, matches, torch, a light bulb, black material, pictures of the moon and stars. Arrange them as a display, perhaps with some candles lit and others unlit.

THINKING ABOUT LIGHT AND DARKNESS

Can you remember any experiences of real, physical darkness when there was no light at all? Examples might be a power cut, camping in the countryside, waking in the night, sleeping in a strange house where no lights were left on, or a cabin without a porthole. How did you feel in each situation? What equipment did you have or need to help you?

Think, too, of experiences of light coming out of darkness. Think about flashes of lightning, fireworks, a lighthouse or a wonderful sunrise. You may have memories of coming into the light from a dark place, or light suddenly being restored after a power failure. How did you feel? What did you do?

THINK OR DISCUSS

- How is coming to know Jesus like coming into the light?
- How will we help Joe and Amy to know Jesus?

SCRIPTURE READING

Here is one of the stories of Jesus healing someone who was blind. This story is different from the others because Jesus used it to teach his followers that he is the light of the world.

As Jesus was walking along, he saw a man who had been born blind. His disciples asked him, 'Teacher, whose sin caused him to be born blind? Was it his own or his parents' sin?'

Jesus answered, 'His blindness has nothing to do with his sins or his parents' sins. He is blind so that God's power might be seen at work in him. As long as it is day, we must keep on doing the work of him who sent me; night is coming when no one can work. While I am in the world, I am the light for the world.'

After he said this, Jesus spat on the ground and made some mud with the spittle; he rubbed the mud on the man's eyes and said, 'Go and wash your face in the Pool of Siloam.' (This name means 'Sent'.) So the man went, washed his face, and came back seeing.

JOHN 9:1–7

TALKING ABOUT LIGHT AND DARKNESS WITH CHILDREN

Before you start, be aware that some children are scared of the dark. Be firm with any child who starts to talk about spooks or monsters.

Set up a simple obstacle course such as two or three chairs in a row. Invite a child to walk around them. Then blindfold the child and ask him or her to follow the course again. Check that the child will not mind being blindfolded before you start the exercise. Promise that you will be there to provide guidance.

Ask the child how he or she felt the first time, and then the second time.

Ask the children if they can remember any time when it was very dark. Examples might be a power cut, night-time in the countryside, waking up very late when no lights were left on, or playing games in the dark. How did they feel? Which of the items on display would they need to help them?

Then talk about light coming out of darkness. Some examples are exciting, like flashes of lightning or fire-works. Some are useful, like traffic lights, car headlights or a lighthouse. Talk about how each one helps us.

THINK OR DISCUSS

- There are many kinds of light and darkness.
- Sometimes we say 'Oh! I see now' when something is explained to us. It does not mean that the light has been turned on, but that we understand something. That is a kind of light coming out of darkness.
- Bad things like theft and murder are sometimes called 'dark deeds'. Can you think why this is?

- How is coming to know Jesus like coming into the light?

Light a candle. Read the story of Jesus healing the man who was born blind from the text above, in your own words, or from a children's version.

Ask the children why they think Jesus called himself the Light of the World.

TALKING WITH JOE

You could use this wording when talking about light and darkness.

'Why do we turn the light on when it is getting dark? We need it to see what we are doing. God gave us light to help us. We have the sun in the day and the moon and stars at night.'

If you get an opportunity, show Joe the sky on a clear night.

IN THE SERVICE

THE DECISION

This part of the baptism service is concerned with turning away from all that is wrong and facing the new life in Christ. When the first Christians were baptized, the ceremony usually took place early in the morning. They stood facing the west. At the words, 'I turn to Christ', they turned around to face the rising sun.

The priest or minister leading the service asks the questions, and the people taking part in the baptism answer with the words printed in bold. The questions are very searching and difficult. Read them together and be prepared to talk about what they mean.

In baptism, God calls us out of darkness into his marvellous light. To follow Christ means dying to sin and rising to new life with him. Therefore, I ask:

Do you reject the devil and all rebellion against God?
I reject them.
Do you renounce the deceit and corruption of evil?
I renounce them.
Do you repent of the sins that separate us from God and neighbour?
I repent of them.

Do you turn to Christ as Saviour?
I turn to Christ.
Do you submit to Christ as Lord?
I submit to Christ.
Do you come to Christ, the way, the truth and the life?
I come to Christ.

AFTER THE BAPTISM

Joe and Amy's parents and godparents made these promises on their behalf. Now it is for them to help Joe and Amy to make the promises their own gradually as they grow up.

On the anniversary of your child's baptism, take a few moments to light the baptismal candle and remember the promises.

PRAYER

Light a single candle. Say together the prayer that follows the decision and signing of the cross in the baptism service.

May Almighty God deliver us from the powers of darkness,
restore us in the image of his glory
and lead us in the light and obedience of Christ. Amen

COMMON WORSHIP: PRAYER AFTER THE SIGNING WITH THE CROSS

Chapter Three

THE GIFT OF THE CROSS

PREPARATION

The two symbols discussed in this chapter are oil and the sign of the cross. Collect and display some of the following items.

- Olive oil, scented oil or the oils that will be used in the baptism service.
- A cross.
- Clothes that have badges on them, like football shirts and a school blazer.

THINKING ABOUT BELONGING

We wear clothes with badges on them to show that we belong to or support a particular organization or team—as signs of loyalty and membership. Most badges have a story attached to them. Football badges are usually connected with the team's name or the place where they play. School badges are often the same, or they may carry the coat of arms of the founder or, in a Church school, the saint after which the school is named.

Wearing a badge brings a sense of responsibility, because it makes the wearer recognizable. We are all ashamed when our football fans misbehave abroad, because they let our country down. School-children are reminded to behave well when they are in uniform because the school is judged by their behaviour.

Joe and Amy will be given invisible 'badges' just before they are baptized. The priest will sign them on the forehead with the sign of the cross. This shows that they belong to Jesus and are part of his family, the Church. Jesus died on the cross to save us. Just as belonging to a school or a club carries responsibilities, so does belonging to Christ. Joe and Amy will gradually learn what it means to be a follower and friend of Jesus for the rest of their lives.

In some churches, the sign of the cross on the forehead will be made with oil. We all need oil to keep us going: olive oil is used in food, cooking, cosmetics, and medicine; fossil oil is used in engines and cars. The 'Oil of Strengthening' may be used to make the sign of the cross before baptism as a sign of strengthening your child to run the Christian race of life—just like an athlete uses embrocation. Your child may be anointed again after baptism with the 'Oil of Blessing' or 'Chrism'. This is a mixture of oil and perfume, used as a sign of God's Holy Spirit being poured out on us at particular turning points of life. This oil is also used at confirmation, ordination of priests and bishops, and coronations.

THINK OR DISCUSS

- What does the sign of the cross mean to you?
- How can we try to live up to that sign?
- How can we help our children to do the same?

This is part of Jesus' teaching to his followers.

Jesus called the crowd and his disciples to him. 'If anyone wants to come with me,' he told them, 'he must forget self, carry his cross, and follow me.'

MARK 8:34

When the apostle Paul wrote to encourage Timothy, one of the early Christian leaders, he described a Christian as being like an athlete in a race.

Run your best in the race of faith, and win eternal life for yourself; for it was to this life that God called you when you firmly professed your faith before many witnesses.

1 TIMOTHY 6:12

TALKING ABOUT BELONGING
WITH CHILDREN

Ask if the children can recognize any of the badges in your display. If any of the children are wearing badges, ask about them too. Draw out the point that we wear badges to show that we belong to or support a particular organization or team.

Most badges have a story attached to them. The children may be able to tell you about their own badges. Football badges are usually connected with the team's name or the place where they play. School badges are often the same, or they may carry the coat of arms of the founder or, in a Church school, the saint after whom the school is named. Scout and Guide badges are symbols of the promise that is made at enrolment.

Wearing a badge tells people whom you support or the name of your school. We have to remember that some people will judge us by the badge we wear. They may also judge our whole school or team by the way that we behave.

Joe and Amy will be given a 'badge' each, just before they are baptized. The priest will sign them on the forehead with the sign of the cross. We cannot see it because it does not leave a mark but it shows that they are friends and followers of Jesus. People cannot see the cross but they will know that we try to follow Jesus by the way we behave.

In some churches, the sign of the cross will be made with oil. This is a sign of strengthening Joe and Amy to run the Christian race of life. They may be anointed again after baptism with the 'Oil of Blessing' or 'Chrism'. This is a mixture of oil and perfume and has been blessed by the bishop. This oil may also be used at confirmation. Queen Elizabeth II was anointed with Chrism at her coronation.

Let the children touch and smell the oil.

THINK OR DISCUSS

- What badges do you wear? What do they show?
- Think of one thing you can do that shows that you are a Christian.

This is one of the things that Jesus taught to his friends.

Jesus called the crowd and his disciples to him. 'If any-one wants to come with me,' he told them, 'he must forget self, carry his cross, and follow me.'

MARK 8:34

❋

TALKING WITH JOE

Most children have clothes with badges on them. Talk about the badges. When you see one with a cross on it, say that Christians wear this badge.

❋

IN THE SERVICE

SIGNING WITH THE CROSS

At the end of the 'decision' part of the service, the priest will make the sign of the cross on Joe and Amy's foreheads, saying:

Christ claims you for his own. Receive the sign of his cross. Do not be ashamed to confess the faith of Christ crucified. Fight valiantly as a disciple of Christ against sin, the world and the devil, and remain faithful to Christ to the end of your life.

AFTER THE BAPTISM

There are many ways of reminding Joe and Amy of the sign of the cross. Many girls, and some boys, wear a cross around their neck or as a lapel badge. They might like to have a cross in their bedrooms. There will be at least one cross or crucifix in your church. Talk about how Jesus died on the cross for us on Good Friday but is now alive. The cross is the sign that we are his followers and friends.

PRAYER

The cross is the sign of our being followers of Jesus, so we say the prayer that he taught us:

Our Father, who art in heaven,
Hallowed be thy name;
Thy kingdom come;
Thy will be done;
On earth as it is in heaven.
Give us this day our daily bread.
And forgive us our trespasses,
As we forgive those who trespass against us.
And lead us not into temptation;
But deliver us from evil.
For thine is the kingdom, the power, and the glory,
For ever and ever. Amen

Chapter Four

THE GIFT OF WATER

PREPARATION

Assemble a collection of items connected with water—for example:

- jug of water with a large bowl
- soap and towel
- watering can
- empty glass
- two plants, one dried up and one green

THINKING ABOUT WATER

Water is vital for life. Nothing can survive without it. We drink it, wash in it and use it to refresh us. Lack of water leads to dirt, disease and death.

Water can also be dangerous. Floods damage livelihoods and property. People can be drowned.

Joe and Amy will be baptized by water being poured over their heads, or maybe by being totally immersed in the water. This symbolizes three things. Think about which articles in your display are linked with each of the three processes.

Cleansing

Water is used in many cultures as a sign of washing away sins and making a fresh start. Baptism is about becoming a Christian, a follower of Jesus Christ. That means turning away from sin—the things in our own lives and in the wider world that are wrong—and accepting the new life in all its fullness that Jesus promised us. Before the baptism, you will be asked to reject all that is evil and to be sorry for the sins that spoil our relationships with God and each other. Joe and Amy are too young to make these promises for themselves, but we can still pray that they will come to know God's forgiveness of sins and the new life that it brings.

New life

Many Christians are baptized by walking down into a pool, going under the water and then out at the other side. This is a sign of new life. It also reminds us that Jesus died, went down into the earth, and then rose again. In baptism, we 'die' to the past and rise to new life as Christians.

Refreshment

Water refreshes us when we are hot and tired. It revives dried-up plants. Jesus said that he would give us 'living water'. He said that people who 'drank from him' would never be thirsty.

The font

The font is like a large bowl. It is traditionally placed near the church door to symbolize that the newly baptized person is entering the Church. It may also be in the centre of the building so that everyone can see the baptism and welcome the new Christian into God's family, the Church. The shape of the font is symbolic: roundness reminds us of the eternity of God, and an octagon shows the seven days of the creation with the eighth side being the resurrection, our new creation. A rectangle is the shape of a grave: in baptism we are buried and then risen with Christ.

THINK OR DISCUSS

- How do we use the various articles that we have assembled?
- How do they link with the reasons we use water in baptism?
- How is baptism a new start for Joe and Amy?

SCRIPTURE READINGS

We read in the Bible that John the Baptist, Jesus' cousin, baptized his followers in the River Jordan as a sign that they had repented of their sins. Although Jesus was sinless, he asked John to baptize him. It was after this that he started his ministry of teaching and healing.

John appeared in the desert, baptizing and preaching. 'Turn away from your sins and be baptized,' he told the people, 'and God will forgive your sins.' ...

Not long afterwards Jesus came from Nazareth in the province of Galilee, and was baptized by John in the Jordan. As soon as Jesus came up out of the water, he saw heaven opening and the Spirit coming down on him like a dove. And a voice came from heaven, 'You are my own dear Son. I am pleased with you.'
MARK 1:4, 9–11

One of the many poems in the Bible likens God's followers to well-watered plants.

Happy are those who reject the advice of evil people,
   who do not follow the example of sinners
   or join those who have no use for God.
Instead they find joy in obeying the Law of the Lord;
   and they study it day and night.
They are like trees that grow beside a stream,
   that bear fruit at the right time,
   and whose leaves do not dry up.

PSALM 1:1–3

TALKING ABOUT WATER WITH CHILDREN

Use these questions to think about the different uses of water.

- When do you like drinking water? What other drinks do you like? Remind the children that every drink is made from water.
- Do you enjoy having a bath or shower? Why should we wash regularly?
- Has anyone planted seeds or watered plants? What happens if it does not rain on them?
- What would happen if we did not have any water? Remind the children that some people do not have enough water.

Joe and Amy will be baptized in a font, which is like a big bowl. Water will be poured over their heads, or they may be completely dipped in the water.

This will be making them clean, like a bath. It will give them a new start as Christians.

It will be refreshing. Water refreshes us when we are hot and thirsty.

It will be a sign of Joe and Amy's new life as friends of Jesus. Water gives life to our plants and trees.

- How do we use the various articles that we have assembled?
- How do they link with the reasons we use water in baptism?
- How is baptism a new start for Joe and Amy?

We read in the Bible that John the Baptist, Jesus' cousin, baptized his followers in the River Jordan. Although Jesus had not done anything wrong, he asked John to baptize him.

John appeared in the desert, baptizing and preaching. 'Turn away from your sins and be baptized,' he told the people, 'and God will forgive your sins.' …

Not long afterwards Jesus came from Nazareth in the province of Galilee, and was baptized by John in the Jordan. As soon as Jesus came up out of the water, he saw heaven opening and the Spirit coming down on him like a dove. And a voice came from heaven, 'You are my own dear Son. I am pleased with you.'

MARK 1:4, 9–11

TALKING WITH JOE

When you are helping Joe to wash in the morning, or before going out, say, 'We wash you to make you clean. Then you can go to pre-school with your friends. You will have water poured on you in church when you are baptized. Then you will be a friend of Jesus.'

When you are watering plants, remind Joe that the plants will die if they have not any water to drink.

✳

IN THE SERVICE

PRAYER OVER THE WATER

You will assemble with Joe and Amy, your family and godparents around the font. The priest or minister will bless the water and then will baptize the children by pouring water three times over their heads. He may use a baptismal shell to hold the water. Large shells were worn by pilgrims as a sign that they were on pilgrimage, a journey to a holy place. The Christian life is a journey that goes through life until we enjoy God's presence in heaven.

AFTER THE BAPTISM

Arrange for Joe and Amy to have an opportunity to see other children being baptized. Point out the font when you go to church. Some churches offer an opportunity to renew baptismal vows at Easter. Others invite people to sprinkle themselves with water from the font or a dish by the church door to remind themselves of their baptism. Let Joe and Amy join in as much of this as they can.

As Joe and Amy get older, help them to own up to wrongdoing and to say sorry to God and to other people. The Christian journey has easy and difficult times and places. See that you support Joe and Amy through them with your prayers, example and help.

PRAYER

We thank you, almighty God,
for the gift of water to sustain, refresh and cleanse all life.

We thank you, Father, for the water of baptism.
In it, we are buried with Christ in his death.
By it, we share in his resurrection.

COMMON WORSHIP: THE PRAYER OVER THE WATER

Chapter Five

THE GIFT OF FAITH

PREPARATION

In this chapter, we are discussing the most demanding part of the baptism service, the profession of faith. Collect and display some of the signs we use to learn about our faith—for example:

- a cross
- a Bible
- a glass bowl or jug containing water
- a candle
- a drawing of a clover leaf or some real clover

THINKING ABOUT FAITH

We cannot explain God. We cannot prove that he exists. When we talk about him, we often tell stories, like those in the Bible. We also use signs and symbols, like the cross, water and light that we have discussed in previous chapters.

The early Christians spent a lot of time trying to find words to explain what Christians believe. Eventually they wrote a statement of faith. This is often called the Creed, from the Latin word *credo*, which means *I believe*. It starts with belief in God the Father who created everything. Then it recalls the life, death and resurrection of Jesus, God's own Son. The last section speaks of God the Holy Spirit, the giver of God's life and power to his people.

There is one God, in three persons. St Patrick used a shamrock (like a small clover leaf) to explain it to his followers. Look at a clover leaf. It is one leaf, but it is also three leaves. We believe in one God, but in three distinct persons: the Father who created everything; the Son, Jesus, who lived and died for us and rose again; and the Holy Spirit who proceeds from both of them. Together, they are called the Holy Trinity.

Another way of demonstrating the Trinity is to draw a triangle with the angles for the Father and the Son at the top, and the Holy Spirit at the bottom.

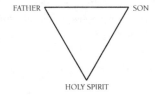

THINK OR DISCUSS

- The Creed was written a long time ago. Why is it still important today?
- The Scripture passage below says that Jesus' closest friends worshipped him but their faith was mingled with doubt. What does this say to us?

These are Jesus' farewell words to his friends before his ascension.

The eleven disciples went to the hill in Galilee where Jesus had told them to go. When they saw him, they worshipped him, even though some of them doubted. Jesus drew near and said to them, 'I have been given all authority in heaven and on earth. Go, then, to all peoples everywhere and make them my disciples: baptize them in the name of the Father, the Son, and the Holy Spirit, and teach them to obey everything I have commanded you. And I will be with you always, to the end of the age.'
MATTHEW 28:16–20

We are carrying on Jesus' command to make disciples by baptizing Joe and Amy. It does not stop there. We have to teach them about the Christian faith. There is a lot to discover. It is rather like starting on a journey that will last the rest of their lives. That is daunting, but Jesus has promised to support us, by being with us 'until the end of time'.

TALKING ABOUT FAITH WITH CHILDREN

Tell the story of St Patrick, using your own words or the words below, or reading from a book of saints. Patrick was taken to Ireland as a slave when he was about sixteen. After six years he escaped and trained to be a priest, probably in Gaul (France). He returned to Ireland as a missionary. He travelled all over Ireland, teaching, and building churches and schools.

People asked him, 'How can God be three and also one?' Patrick took a shamrock leaf and said, 'Here is one leaf, but it is also three leaves. We worship three persons in one God: the Father, Son, and Holy Spirit.' The shamrock is still the Irish national emblem, and is worn on St Patrick's day, 17 March.

- Make some patterns using the clover leaf shape.
- When Joe and Amy are baptized, it will be 'in the name of the Father, and of the Son, and of the Holy Spirit'. Listen for other times when you hear those words spoken, and remember the Holy Trinity, three persons in one God.

SCRIPTURE READING

Link the story of Patrick to the Bible reading when Jesus gives his last command to his friends:

'Go, then, to all peoples everywhere and make them my disciples: baptize them in the name of the Father, the Son, and the Holy Spirit, and teach them to obey everything I have commanded you. And I will be with you always, to the end of the age.'

MATTHEW 28:19–20

✳

TALKING WITH JOE

Next time you are in a park or field, look in the grass for clover. Show Joe how each leaf is also three little leaves. When Joe is older, tell him the story of St Patrick and remind him what the clover leaf looks like.

✳

IN THE SERVICE

THE PROFESSION OF FAITH

The priest or minister will ask everyone present to join with you in the profession of faith. This is often called the Creed, from the Latin word *credo*, meaning 'I believe'. It is asking you to affirm that you believe in:

- God as the creator of the universe, who we call our Father.
- God's Son, Jesus, who lived among us, and died and rose again for us.
- God's Holy Spirit, who lives within us and empowers us to carry on Jesus' saving work.

This is known as the Holy Trinity.

AFTER THE BAPTISM

Mark the occasion by giving a card on each anniversary of the child's baptism. If the church where the baptism took place sends cards, talk to Joe and Amy about the cards to show that you value them.

PRAYER

I bind unto myself the name,
The strong name of the Trinity
By invocation of the same,
The Three in One and One in Three
Of whom all nature hath creation;
Eternal Father, Spirit, Word:
Praise to the Lord of my salvation,
Salvation is of Christ the Lord.

ST PATRICK (c.390–461)

Chapter Six

THE GIFT OF NEW LIFE

PREPARATION

Ideally, you should read this chapter in the church or soon after a visit to the church where Joe and Amy are to be baptized. Stand by the font. You will remember from Chapter Four, 'The gift of water', that it is usually placed near the church door to symbolize that the newly baptized person is entering the Church. It may also be in the centre of the building so that everyone can see the baptism and welcome the new Christian into the midst of God's family, the Church.

If you are not able to visit the church, fill a bowl with water to remind you of the font where Joe and Amy will be baptized.

THINKING ABOUT BAPTISM

This is the central part of the baptism service. You have asked for Joe and Amy to be baptized. This is the moment when your request is granted. Part of bringing up children is gradually letting them go. You will hand Joe and Amy to the priest or minister. You are offering them back to God. You are also allowing God to act in them as they start on life's pilgrimage. When they are baptized, your children will be addressed by their names, their Christian names. This reminds us that God knows us as individuals and calls each one of us by our names. We belong to him and we can call him our Father.

THINK OR DISCUSS

Use this opportunity to think through the reasons you have asked for Joe and Amy to be baptized.

- Have your views altered since you took this step?
- Do you have any new questions about what baptism means? If so, speak to the priest or minister who will be leading the baptism service.

SCRIPTURE READING

When the Jewish people were in exile in Babylon, the prophet Isaiah described the return from exile as a new creation. The Jewish people were God's people. He would call them by name, bring them through the dangers of fire and water and take them home to Jerusalem, to begin a new life.

The Lord who created you says, 'Do not be afraid—I will save you. I have called you by name—you are mine. When you pass through deep waters, I will be with you; your troubles will not overwhelm you. When you pass through fire, you will not be burnt; the hard trials that come will not hurt you. For I am the Lord your God, the holy God of Israel, who saves you.'
ISAIAH 43:1–3A

In a letter that Paul wrote to the Christians in Galatia, he explains that baptism is uniting us with Christ. We are all God's children.

In some Greek religions, the initiation ceremony involved the person identifying himself with a god by putting on his robes. Paul uses this idea to illustrate that we 'put on Christ' as if he were a new garment.

You were baptized into union with Christ, and now you are clothed, so to speak, with the life of Christ himself.

GALATIANS 3:27

TALKING ABOUT BAPTISM WITH CHILDREN

Prepare the discussion by presenting a bowl of water and a doll. Remind the children about the story of Jesus being baptized (see Chapter Four, 'The gift of water'). Using the bowl of water and the doll, show how a baby is baptized. Pour the water over the doll's head three times with the words, '(Name) I baptize you in the name of the Father, and of the Son, and of the Holy Spirit. Amen.' You could ask the children to contribute to the demonstration by choosing a name for the doll and being 'parents' and 'godparents'.

THINK OR DISCUSS

* Being baptized is a bit like having a bath to get us clean. What can happen if we are not clean?
* When we are baptized, the priest or minister uses our names. This is to show that God knows each of us individually and calls us by our names. How does that make us feel?
* Each one of us is special. God loves us and is with us all the time. When is it helpful to remember that?

Long before Jesus was born, the prophet Isaiah told the children of Israel that God promised to be with them through their difficulties. He said:

'Do not be afraid—I will save you. I have called you by name—you are mine. When you pass through deep waters, I will be with you; your troubles will not overwhelm you… the hard trials that come will not hurt you. For I am the Lord your God, the holy God of Israel, who saves you.

ISAIAH 43:1–3A

✳

TALKING WITH JOE

Practise Joe's baptism at home by pouring a little water on his head while he leans over the washbasin. Use very little water and wipe it off so that he does not get wet. Before the baptismal service, you will probably have a rehearsal. Make sure that Joe has seen the font, climbed up and had a good look at it, so that he knows exactly what is going to happen.

✳

IN THE SERVICE

THE BAPTISM

The priest or minister will lift Amy up and pour water over her head three times, saying, *'Amy, I baptize you in the name of the Father, and of the Son, and of the Holy Spirit. Amen.'* He or she may use a large shell for the water. The shell is a sign of pilgrimage. This reminds us that Amy is starting on a journey as a Christian.

As Joe is four, he will probably be asked to stand on a stool and lean forward over the font, or he may be lifted up and asked to lean forward.

People being baptized usually wear white as a sign of cleansing and new life. Occasionally, they put on a white garment after the baptism while saying or hearing the words based on Paul's letter that we have just read: 'You have been clothed with Christ. As many as are baptized into Christ have put on Christ.'

AFTER THE BAPTISM

Take some photographs of Joe and Amy. Bring them out and talk about them on each anniversary.

PRAYER

May God, who will receive Joe and Amy by baptism into his Church,
pour upon them the riches of his grace,
that within the company of Christ's pilgrim people
they may daily be renewed by his anointing spirit
and come to the inheritance of the saints in glory. Amen

COMMON WORSHIP

Chapter Seven

THE GIFT OF GLORY

PREPARATION

The world is full of God's glory. We have glimpses of it in beautiful things. Collect a few objects that show the glory of God by their beauty—flowers, shells, pebbles and so on.

THINKING ABOUT WORSHIP

This chapter explores Joe and Amy's relationship with God. Just as they will grow physically and mentally, they will also grow spiritually. We hope that they will grow to know God. They will meet him through worship, prayer, other people, and the beauty of creation. Our duty is to help them to recognize God in all these things.

Joe and Amy should learn to worship God with other Christians. Unless they go to a Church school, you cannot guarantee that they will learn much about the Christian faith at school. Your local church is there to support you in nurturing your children. It will probably have a Junior Church or Sunday school. It may also have a parent and toddler group that includes simple worship, or a monthly family service. Be prepared to visit churches near where you live to find one that caters for children, or contact your Diocesan office for advice.

THINK OR DISCUSS

- Can you remember a special time when you had a glimpse of God's glory through something unusual or beautiful? It may have been something like a rainbow, or it could have been a person or an event. These times can lead us towards being aware of the presence of God and worshipping him.
- Sometimes we are so thankful for something, or so desperate, that we pray almost without realizing it. That prayer might be just, 'Help!'
- Most of us find prayer difficult at times. Discuss things that might help us to start praying and help Joe and Amy to pray.

SCRIPTURE READING

Jesus took with him Peter, James, and John, and led them up a high mountain, where they were alone. As they looked on, a change came over Jesus, and his clothes became shining white—whiter than anyone in the world could wash them...

Then a cloud appeared and covered them with its shadow, and a voice came from the cloud, 'This is my own dear Son—listen to him!'

MARK 9:2–3, 7

TALKING ABOUT WORSHIP WITH CHILDREN

Talk about special times when the children have had a glimpse of God's glory in the world. These times can lead us towards being aware of the presence of God and worshipping him.

THINK OR DISCUSS

- When have you experienced something very beautiful or special in God's creation?
- What reminds you of God's love for you?
- It is not always easy to remember that God is with us. What can we use to help us?

SCRIPTURE READING

Tell the story of the transfiguration, from the above version, or in your own words, or from a children's Bible.

TALKING WITH JOE

When you go out for a walk or are in the garden or a park, help Joe to take in the wonder of God's creation. Encourage him to look, listen, smell and, if appropriate, touch things. Young children have a natural sense of awe and wonder. We need to encourage it to grow so that they do not lose it.

IN THE SERVICE

THE COMMISSION

A minister will remind you of your duty to bring up Joe and Amy in the Christian faith. He will then say a prayer for God's grace to support you in this task.

AFTER THE BAPTISM

Include Christian songs with any others that you may sing. 'All things bright and beautiful' was written especially to help children to worship God. There are illustrated books of children's hymns or songs.

A simple first prayer can be 'Thank you, God, for everything'. Help Joe to make it his own prayer by saying, 'Thank you, God, for…' and letting him finish the sentence as he wishes. Let Amy share in prayer time and join in as she learns to talk.

PRAYER

God of grace and life,
In your love you have given us
a place among your people;
Keep us faithful to our baptism,
and prepare us for the glorious day
when the whole creation will be made perfect
in your son our Saviour Jesus Christ. Amen

COMMON WORSHIP: PRAYER FROM THE COMMISSION

Chapter Eight

THE GIFT OF THE CHURCH

PREPARATION

In this chapter, we are discussing what we mean by 'Church'. The immediate answer would probably be that it is a building where Christians worship God. We are going to focus on two other aspects —those of a journey, and of a family or body. As aids to your thinking or discussion, collect and display:

- a road map
- a compass, if you can find one
- a small jigsaw puzzle in pieces

THINKING ABOUT THE CHURCH

In previous chapters, we have thought about Joe and Amy becoming part of God's family, the Church, when they are baptized. We have also thought of their Christian life being like a journey. In the chapter about the actual baptism, we noted that the ceremony traditionally takes place at the church door, to symbolize that Joe and Amy are entering the Church. It is clear that it is not just a building, or even a group of people who meet there. The members of the Church live in every part of the world and belong to every age and time. The first members were Jesus' friends, there have been Christians through every century and there are those who are still to be born. We are united in Christ by our faith and our baptism.

Imagine being on a long walk with your friends. Some of you walk fast. Other people stop to look at things. Some people, because they are very young or very old, need help. Children run ahead and then get tired. Leaders will point the way; teachers will explain things about what we see. Helpers will provide food and even first aid. Perhaps the Church is a bit like that. We are all on a journey. We travel together, but at our own pace, with fellow Christians to help us on our way. They are like the map and the compass. The signs on the map tell us about the journey. The compass tells us in which direction we are travelling. Spend a few minutes thinking about things you can see on the map.

You and your children are welcome to be part of that journey. Everyone has something to offer to God's family, the Church. It is like the pieces in the jigsaw. All the pieces are important. Take a piece or two of the puzzle and fit them together. Think about how much easier it would be to make the picture if you were working along with others. You and your children are welcome to make your contribution to the picture of the Church.

THINK OR DISCUSS

- Who and what can help Joe and Amy on their Christian journey?
- How can we as parents and godparents be involved?
- We thought about helping each other to make the jigsaw picture. Has this altered our view of the Church?
- On our Christian journeys we have the support of our fellow Christians. We also have the power of God's Spirit acting in our lives. How does that make us feel?
- Is there anything else that we want to know?

The world is full of different religions, cults and beliefs. If you have visited churches for friends' weddings and baptisms, you will have seen different styles and traditions of Christian worship. You may have friends who belong to other faiths. The people of Ephesus in the first century also came from a variety of religious backgrounds. Paul wrote a letter to them to remind them of the unity that distinguishes the Christian life—the same God, the same teachings, and the same new life entered into at baptism.

There is one body and one Spirit, just as there is one hope to which God has called you. There is one Lord, one faith, one baptism; there is one God and Father of all, who is Lord of all, works through all, and is in all.

EPHESIANS 4:4–6

Paul also describes the Church as being like a body, made up of many parts. Its members work together for the common good of the community.

We have many parts in the one body, and all these parts have different functions. In the same way, though we are many, we are one body in union with Christ, and we are all joined to each other as different parts of one body. So we are to use our different gifts in accordance with the grace that God has given us. If our gift is to speak God's message, we should do it according to the faith that we have; if it is to serve, we should serve; if it is to teach, we should teach; if it is to encourage others, we should do so.

ROMANS 12:4–8A

Joe and Amy may be baptized in a small chapel, a village church, or a huge cathedral. The service may be simple and last about twenty minutes. It may be part of the main Sunday service and be full of ceremonial. Joe and Amy will become baptized Christians, part of

God's family, his universal Church. However we express it, we are in union with Jesus, like parts of a body or parts of a jigsaw puzzle. Each one of us can have a part to play.

TALKING ABOUT THE CHURCH
WITH CHILDREN

Prepare for this discussion by drawing around the smallest person in the group. Cut out the shape and then cut it into pieces like a jigsaw.

Ask the children to tell you things that they or their friends are good at doing. They will probably talk about achievements at school. Include other gifts like helping, listening, being cheerful, and welcoming new children to the group.

Give a piece of the jigsaw to each child. Ask them to write their names and gifts on their piece. If there are spare pieces, ask them to write someone else's name and gifts on a second piece. Then put the pieces together to make a body. Show how you need all the parts of the body to make the figure complete. Explain that the Church is like a body. Every person and gift matters. God values each of us and has a job for us to do, however small it may seem.

THINK OR DISCUSS

- Do I have gifts I can use to help people or make them happy?
- Do I welcome new people to the group?
- Do I realize that everyone in the church is important to God?

SCRIPTURE READING

Read how Paul explains to his friends that, just as each part of our bodies has a different job (the eyes to see and feet to walk), so each member of the church has a different job to do.

We have many parts in the one body, and all these parts have different functions. In the same way, though we are many, we are one body in union with Christ, and we are all joined to each other as different parts of one body. So we are to use our different gifts in accordance with the grace that God has given us.

ROMANS 12:4–6

TALKING WITH JOE

Make sure that Joe's toys include simple jigsaw puzzles. He will soon learn that the picture is incomplete if one piece is missing. As he and Amy get older, they will learn how members of the family help each other and have their own gifts and skills. It is the same with the Christian family.

IN THE SERVICE

THE WELCOME

At the end of the baptism, the people assembled will formally welcome the newest members of the Christian family. The priest or

minister may use some of Paul's letter to the Christians in Ephesus
that we have just read:

There is one Lord, one faith, one baptism:
Joe and Amy, by one Spirit we are all baptized into one body.

Then everyone will join in by saying:

We welcome you into the fellowship of faith;
We are children of the same heavenly Father;
We welcome you.

AFTER THE BAPTISM

Make sure that their toys, videos, and books include some that
reflect Christian values. When Joe and Amy watch television, be
ready to talk about the programmes and the way that people treat
each other in them.

PRAYER

Pour your blessing on all your people.
May our hearts ever praise you,
And find their perfect rest in you.
Grant us the freedom of your service
And peace in doing your will.

Father of life,
Make known your glory.

COMMON WORSHIP: ALTERNATIVE PRAYERS OF INTERCESSION

Postscript

THE GIFT OF THE WORLD

AFTER THE BAPTISM

It is Sunday evening. The last of the guests have departed. Amy is asleep in her crib. Joe is in his bed, but still awake. The events of the last few days are still in his mind.

Yesterday they had been to St Mary's for a rehearsal. The church looked different when there were only a few people there. He had sat in the front row with his parents, and with Uncle John, Auntie Ruth and Simon, his Sunday Club leader, who were going to be his godparents. Mum had explained that they were going to help him to grow up to follow Jesus. Joe knew about Jesus now. Simon had told him.

The vicar, Tim, was there. He showed them places to stand. Everyone practised making a mark like a cross on Amy's forehead. She had stayed asleep. Then they did it to Joe. It tickled. Everyone laughed when he rubbed the spot. Then they had all lined up as they did at preschool and walked to the back of the church. Tim asked Joe to climb on to a stool and lean over the font. Dad steadied him. It looked like a big washbasin. It was all a bit strange but everybody said that he was being really good.

The next morning, Joe had been dressed in his new white shirt and blue trousers. He felt very smart. Amy looked pretty in a long white dress. When they arrived at St Mary's everyone was smiling at them. Tim said, 'We are going to welcome Joe and Amy into God's family. We are pleased that they are here with their family and friends.' Then they all stood at the front. Dad held Joe's hand tightly. There was a lot of talking. Then Tim made a cross on Joe's forehead with oil. This time it did not tickle. As they walked to the back of the church, the organ played grand music and everyone sang. It sounded wonderful.

They stood by the font. There were all Joe's new friends from the Sunday Club standing there. Carol from the preschool was there too. Jason waved to him. Then Tim took Amy in his arms and poured water over her head. He said, 'Amy Rose, I baptize you in the name of the Father, and of the Son, and of the Holy Spirit.' Amy woke up and cried a bit. Joe wondered if she was hurt, but she stopped and just looked around. Tim held her up for everyone to see.

Then it was Joe's turn. He climbed on to the stool. Tim poured the water over his head. It was cold but it did not get into his eyes. Joe heard him say, 'Joseph William, I baptize you in the name of the Father, and of the Son, and of the Holy Spirit.' Then Tim mopped Joe's head. Suddenly he lifted Joe up in the air. Joe could see over everyone's heads. He could see right down the church to the cross and candles on the altar. He could see the picture of Jesus holding out his hands to him in the big coloured window. Everyone was smiling at him. They said, 'We welcome you!' Everyone clapped. Joe felt very special.

Later there was a party at Joe's house, with a big cake. Tim gave Joe a card with a picture of Jesus on it. John and Ruth had given him a big storybook called a Bible, and a silver mug. Amy got a little silver bracelet. They each had a big candle. John and Ruth had held them when they processed out of church at the end of the service.

'See you at Sunday Club,' said Simon as he left. Tim was explaining to Joe's mum that she could take Amy to a pram service on Tuesday. He gave her a piece of paper. 'This will tell you what we do. Just ring me up if you need to know anything.'

Joe is still not quite sure what happened. He knows that he is a friend of Jesus and that God loves him. He likes going to Sunday Club. The church is rather big and dark but the coloured windows and music are nice. Everything seems a bit different. Joe smiles. 'Mum,' he calls, 'can we go to church again tomorrow?'

PRAYER

PATTERN OF LIFE

Through every minute of this day,
be with me Lord!
Through every day of all this week,
be with me Lord!
Through every week of all this year,
be with me Lord!
Through all the years of all this life,
be with me Lord!
So shall the days and weeks and years
be threaded on a golden cord.
And all draw on with sweet accord
unto thy fullness, Lord,
that so, when time is past,
by grace I may at last,
be with thee, Lord.

JOHN OXENHAM (1853–1941)

OTHER RESOURCES
FROM BARNABAS

REF 1 84101 186 X, £8.99

This book gives a comprehensive guide to the Church—its tradition and its faith. Building on *My Book of Special Times in Church* and *My Book of Special Times of Year*, it gives clear and accurate information about the major seasons of the Church year, forms of worship, doctrine and ways in which Christians use prayer. Each of the 28 units sets out key background information and relevant Bible passages and gives practical ideas for learning through activity-based extension material. Photocopy permission is given on activity pages where appropriate.